DON'T BE THE A-HOLE ON THE TEAM

36 Tips to Manage Better and Lead Well

Other Titles By Karl Bimshas

"So, I've Been Thinking"

"Leaders Don't Shrug"

"GO GET IT!"

"Pushing Back the Ocean"

"How to Stay When You Want to Quit"

"Disposable Journal"

"Write Advice"

"Perspectives"

DON'T BE THE A-HOLE ON THE TEAM

36 *Tips to Manage Better and Lead Well*

Karl Bimshas

BimMedia

San Diego, California

First Printing 2018

Karl Bimshas Consulting
7676 Hazard Center Drive, Suite 500
San Diego, CA 92108

www.KarlBimshasConsulting.com

ISBN: 978-0-359-16527-8

DEDICATION

*For new and established leaders who practice servant
leadership and want to be great, not lousy.*

TABLE OF CONTENTS

INTRODUCTION..9

CREATE AND NURTURE CULTURE...13

LEAD PEOPLE FROM "A-HA" TO "NO-DUH."..15

BE THE ONE WHO DOES NOT PANIC...17

REWARD THE EFFORTS OF OTHERS..19

GIVE CONTINUOUS FEEDBACK...21

PLACE TEAM MEMBERS WHERE THEY CAN WIN...23

LEAD PEOPLE WHO DISAGREE WITH YOU...25

DEMONSTRATE EMPATHY...27

TEACH OTHERS...29

BE HONEST..31

SERVE THOSE YOU LEAD...33

PRAISE PROGRESS...35

PROVIDE TOOLS..37

START TO GIVE A C.R.A.P..39

FOCUS ON THE RIGHT THINGS...41

MEET ONE-ON-ONE..43

REMOVE OBSTACLES...45

LOOK IN THE MIRROR..47

FIND WHAT'S RIGHT...49

BE DELIBERATE WITH YOUR INTENTIONS...51

STOP DOING DUMB THINGS..53

ACKNOWLEDGE THAT YOU MIGHT BE WRONG..55

COMMUNICATE YOUR PLAN FREQUENTLY...57

PRODUCE MORE THAN YOU CONSUME...59

SIMPLIFY...61

WORK ON YOURSELF, TOO...63

REMEMBER YOUR A GAME...65

KNOW THE IMPLICATIONS..67

ALWAYS HAVE AN OBJECTIVE..69

KEEP WALLOWING TO 5 MINUTES OR LESS...71

DISTRIBUTE A D.A.M.N. AGENDA..73

PROPERLY HONOR THE PROCESSES YOU KILL..75

FEEDBACK IS A TOOL..77

LEARN WHY PEOPLE LEAVE YOU..79

CULTURE IS CREATED BY THE BEHAVIOR YOU TOLERATE.........................81

BUILD EVERY DAY...83

FINAL TOUGHTS...85

About the Author..87

INTRODUCTION

Leading a team can be equally daunting and fulfilling. Unfortunately, the odds are stacked against most because typically, those who rise in positional power didn't get there for their team prowess.

The gag-inducing personal development trope, "There's no I in team," tried to make the point that there is more power in joint efforts. The saying has greatly diminished after someone found the I hidden within the letter A.

Yet, executive suites and corner offices remain havens for barrel-chested man-babies who treat people like they are disposable.

To be fair, whenever people come together for a common purpose, there will be those who are unwilling to participate fully. Sometimes they are the adored mavericks, the rebel, or the disruptor. I support all those roles, but it is possible to fulfill them without being the a-hole on the team. This guide gives you 36 tips.

You do not need positional power to lead well. Still, many people are ignoring the essential leadership tools that focus on the people that make teams possible. Trying to become a good team leader without being an a-hole can be difficult. Difficulty is not a sufficient excuse for incompetence, and as you know, if you have ever worked for a lousy boss, incompetence not only hurts, it can derail careers.

Leading a team of any size is an important responsibility. Doing it well requires the right mindset and disciplined self-leadership. Use this guide as a preventative measure. Adopt several of the tips and methods discussed, and you will be well on your way to managing better and leading well.

Tip 1

CREATE AND NURTURE CULTURE

The larger the organization, the more defined (and entrenched) the culture. Regardless of the size of the team, leaders set the tone of what is acceptable and what is not. Acknowledge that, like it or not, as a leader, you are a role model. Your actions are being scrutinized and mimicked. Therefore, make sure they reinforce the culture of performance you want.

Tip 2

LEAD PEOPLE FROM "A-HA" TO "NO-DUH."

When faced with something new it is safe to assume people don't know things at first. Connect the dots for them and do it repeatedly. Sometimes, you will feel like you are caught in an endless loop, and your work colleagues still will not "get" something. When you continue to repeat your message, they will eventually understand, perhaps roll their eyes, and say something like, "Everybody knows that." Only then will you know you've succeeded.

Tip 3

BE THE ONE WHO DOES NOT PANIC

Panic is the opposite of leadership.

Panicking does not help you or the people who look to you for guidance. You can be calm, forceful, and clear, and still, lead. Do not be the hothead, the shrill voice, or the man-baby crying for attention. When a crisis arises, rise to meet it with detached confidence. This is not always easy, but it is what you do when you are committed to leading well.

Tip 4

REWARD THE EFFORTS OF
OTHERS

Author, management expert, and mentor, Ken Blanchard is fond of saying, "Raise your hand if you are getting too much reward and recognition." Hands seldom go up. Make a point of noticing what people do right (or approximately right) today, and acknowledge them.

Tip 5

GIVE CONTINUOUS FEEDBACK

Feedback is information. It is not inherently positive or negative - but how it is delivered influences how it is received. First, ask if your feedback would be welcomed, and then be sure what you share is for the benefit of the recipient, not you.

Tip 6

PLACE TEAM MEMBERS WHERE THEY CAN WIN

The point of a team is to accomplish results better than if pursued singularly. Evaluate your current results and decide if you have the right people in the right positions for right now.

Tip 7

LEAD PEOPLE WHO DISAGREE WITH YOU

Leading a group of yes-men is not particularly impressive. There is a skill required to lead effectively, and this approach demonstrates very little mastery. If you rely on positional power and authoritarian tactics, you will attract the weak-willed who will fawn over you. That is not a difficult feat, and your results will be suboptimal.

It is better to be the type of leader who can influence, inspire, and compromise with those who disagree with you. To do so shows your ability to listen, empathize, negotiate, and collaborate. Disagreements do not have to be adversarial. Curiosity can just as easily fuel them. Curiosity is a desirable trait most people enjoy seeing in others.

If you are going to lead, make it worthwhile. Invite challengers to help you clear the obstacles in areas you may not see. They will develop your strengths, and your mutual respect will move everyone closer to the desired vision.

Tip 8

DEMONSTRATE EMPATHY

It is tempting to think of yourself first; after all, you are the person you spend the most time with. Make an effort to understand where another person is coming from. Resist being ego-driven and defensive. Instead, listen, show compassion, and cry unapologetically if you must. Be there for someone besides yourself.

Tip 9

TEACH OTHERS

Sharing your skills and knowledge is a selfless act. Make the extra effort and take the needed time to share a skill, a shortcut, your wisdom gained, or a trick of the trade that will make an invaluable impact on someone else.

Tip 10

BE HONEST

Being honest isn't always painless, but it is easier. When you trade truthfulness for expediency, you chip away at your integrity. Do it often enough, and your integrity will reduce to rubble. You will be left rudderless and subject to the whims of others without any control or direction of your own. Instead of a strong vision, you will be dependent on wishes. You'll chase the current and winds produced by others, instead of your own. You abdicate leadership. It's not worth it. Protect your integrity.

Tip 11

SERVE THOSE YOU LEAD

It is not about you. The team is not there for the career betterment or aggrandization of the leader. It is the reverse. Determine how you will serve your team so they can achieve increasingly more significant things.

Tip 12

PRAISE PROGRESS

Who will you go out of your way to praise today? You might think someone is doing a good job, but telling him or her makes all the difference. Say it. Let someone feel recognized because they matter, what he or she are doing matters, and they are making a difference. Authentically praising people IS your job.

Tip 13

PROVIDE TOOLS

Does your team have the tools they need to succeed? If you are fortunate enough to have a team helping you achieve your goals, make sure you equip them with tools for success. It could be training, reducing bureaucracy, or an adequate supply of red pens. Anything that stands in the way of their success is your responsibility. Always find ways to remove their obstacles.

Tip 14

START TO GIVE A C.R.A.P.

On average, 50-65% of managers do not give a crap. Managers do not care about their direct reports, the organization that pays them, and they do not particularly care about you: their leader. Now, if you are a jackhole like them, maybe you don't care either and if that is the case, look forward to the eventual demise of your organization.

If you DO care, start giving a crap.

- CARE - Care about your direct reports, your clients, and your boss. If you do not, you are doing your job wrong. Either improve or resign from your position.

- RECOGNIZE – If you cannot make the time to recognize people who are helping you achieve the goals you are responsible for, find ways to return to being an individual contributor, because you are not demonstrating a basic component of effective leadership.

- ACCOUNTABILITY – The challenging person to hold accountable is you. You make and break promises to yourself all the time. Polish your integrity. Honor your commitments and your mistakes. Instead of passing blame, accept and fix a problem.

- PERSIST – Do not abdicate your leadership when it gets too hard or uncomfortable. Persist. Don't succumb to apathy when things do not immediately go your way. Persist.

There are plenty of strong, effective leaders. Unfortunately, many effective leaders do not hold positional power. That's okay. Strong leadership has never needed a title. It is most attracted to those who give a crap.

Tip 15

FOCUS ON THE RIGHT THINGS

Make sure you focus on the right things.

Ensure your employees feel valued, so they ensure your customers feel valued because if your customers do not feel valued, you lose. When you lead, you serve your customer, client, patient, member, constituent, or user, not the other way around.

Tip 16

MEET ONE-ON-ONE

Either find the time to have meaningful and regularly scheduled one-on-one meetings with members of your team, or reconsider how you use the word "manager." If you cannot find the time to sit down with your team individually and learn more about their needs, obstacles, ideas, and status on their goals, you need to reevaluate where you are spending your time and begin to make adjustments - fast.

Tip 17

REMOVE OBSTACLES

Roll up your sleeves and genuinely help your team today. Make time to listen, remove their obstacles, and sing their praises. If you cannot make the time to consider your team, work on your time management skills. If you cannot be bothered, it would be best to reevaluate the utility of your role.

Tip 18

LOOK IN THE MIRROR

Your environment is a mirror of what you have created; want a different view? Start with you. You can argue about whether your external environment matches your internal thoughts, or if your inner thoughts create your exterior results, the bottom line is, they are linked closely enough to influence each other. If you do not like the environment you have created, change your surroundings.

Tip 19

FIND WHAT'S RIGHT

Today, find what's right, or approximately right, and praise progress. Do not cast a blind eye to mistakes, but do not provide them with more attention than all the achievements, big or small, you have made along the way.

Tip 20

BE DELIBERATE WITH YOUR INTENTIONS

The best intentions are still only intentions. To make an impact, you have to actually do something. Plan your intentions by asking yourself, *"What do I want to achieve?"* Then give deliberate thought to the following.

- How will doing so make a big difference

- What does success look like?

- Describe the feelings and impact on confidence, beliefs, finances, and other factors?

- Who else will be impacted?

Go deeper with two more questions.
- What is the worst-case scenario?
- What is the best-case scenario?

Don't stop at making your intention,
which is no different from a wish.
Instead, make it happen!

Tip 21

STOP DOING DUMB THINGS

Find a process or system that everyone agrees has outlived its usefulness and put it to an end. Either stop it quietly and see if anyone notices, or have a big funeral to bury it. Remember, every solution creates another problem, so make sure you upgrade your problems.

Tip 22

ACKNOWLEDGE THAT YOU MIGHT BE WRONG

Do not get so hung up on your "truth" that you miss everyone else's reality. The world is full of disinformation. It's not a new phenomenon. Information is just more accessible. While it is crucial that you live an authentic life and act congruent with your values, do not insist that your path is the only correct one. Your life values are not necessarily the easiest, or most difficult, wisest or even economically sensible for anyone but you. Don't be blind to the personal experiences of others.

Tip 23

COMMUNICATE YOUR PLAN
FREQUENTLY

Telepathy doesn't cut it. If you like planning, you spend a lot of time on your plans -- more than anyone else does. So, it's easy to forget that other people may have no idea what you are trying to achieve because they are not in your head. Communicate, in many ways over many days.

Tip 24

PRODUCE MORE THAN YOU
CONSUME

Do more than expected. Not for the money, for the mind. Share your time, treasure, and talent with others. Be a bigger contributor to causes you believe in and the people who support them. They are worth it.

Tip 25

SIMPLIFY

Make things easier, clearer, and more efficient wherever you can. Replace a presentation with an infographic. Draw a picture to illustrate a complex concept. Eliminate redundant steps. Simplify. Simplify. Simplify.

Tip 26

WORK ON YOURSELF, TOO

You are devoted to efficiency, better productivity, and results. Do not exempt yourself from the calculation. You may be a hindrance, either through ignorance or intent. Ponder your motives and skills and make an adjustment to yourself.

Tip 27

REMEMBER YOUR A GAME

Make sure your attitude, appearance, and approach are aligned. Do not confuse people. Your attitude must be appropriate to the task. Your appearance, your attire, and grooming matter more than you would like to think. Your approach and demeanor speak volumes before you open your mouth. Ensure all these elements are aligned with each other and your purpose. Always.

Tip 28

KNOW THE IMPLICATIONS

Work through the implications of your actions, preferably while they are still notions. Lousy leaders act without thought or think without acting. Effective leaders strike the right balance. Every action has consequences, some good, some bad, intended and unintended. Consider your actions without falling into over-analysis.

Tip 29

ALWAYS HAVE AN OBJECTIVE

Act with purpose, every time. When you know your objective and purpose, you improve your execution and are less likely to fall prey to distractions or low impact activity. For every meeting, interaction, and goal, have an objective and work toward its completion.

Tip 30

KEEP WALLOWING TO 5 MINUTES
OR LESS

Do not tolerate wallowing in yourself or your team.

• We wallow when we are feeling relaxed or lazy. Lazy does not pay well, action does.

• We wallow in our victory and success, forgetting how short-lived they can be without vigilance and maintenance.

• We wallow in our failures, giving too much oxygen to our shortcomings and short-shift to our ability to persevere.

Do not deny the emotion that brings about the urge to wallow. Instead, acknowledge it, appreciate it, and then get back to focusing on your purpose.

Tip 31

DISTRIBUTE A D.A.M.N. AGENDA

Complaining about meetings is cliché.
"They feel like a waste of time and
resource." Blah, blah. They ARE if you do
not run them correctly. If you called the
meeting, pull yourself together and act like
a professional.

Every meeting run by an effective leader
has a clear purpose stated up front;
otherwise, there is no point.

- An agenda establishes a purpose. Use
  whatever format works for your
  organization.

- Use a similar format for one-off meetings,
  standing meetings, and client
  presentations, every time.

- Stating a purpose forces you to be
  succinct and keeps you focused.

Parts of a D.A.M.N. Agenda

- Dates - of the meeting, and milestones you are working toward.

- Actions - commitments made or required.

- Motivations - what is the point of the meeting, subtopics, and who beyond you cares?

- Names - of those invited, who attended, who is to be informed and who is accountable for the actions.

Tip 32

PROPERLY HONOR THE
PROCESSES YOU KILL

When you find inefficiency, redundancy, antiquated process, policies, or practices, take a moment to respect their heritage. Many systems that have worn past their usefulness were at one time designed to solve a problem, speed things up, ensure quality, or some other noble purpose.

Do not merely eradicate a given system and move on, honor its contribution with a ceremony of sorts. Involve the team, perhaps members who created the system, to give it a proper send off. Old systems were once heroes. Appreciate the contributions, while making clear, it is time to turn the page. Allow people to mourn the loss and then begin anew.

Tip 33

FEEDBACK IS A TOOL

Resolve to stop being stingy with feedback. Feedback is essential. Make it fast, frequent, relevant, and positively delivered. People tend to hold off on providing feedback as if it were a secret -- that's no good. Holding off dilutes the effectiveness over time, or worse, creates a vacuum. It is much better to provide feedback right then and there. The closer to the event the better. Effective leaders are masters at providing, receiving, discerning, and integrating feedback.

Tip 34

LEARN WHY PEOPLE LEAVE YOU

People move on. Priorities change and conditions ebb and flow. The makeup of your team will vary over time. Pay attention to what attracts people to you: Is it your reputation, your results, your humor, your empathy? Double down on your findings. More importantly, find out why people leave. For the vast majority, it is because of the boss. Are you or your leaders driving people away? Odds are, regardless of all the reasons you collect; they are excuses covering your behavior. Are you acting in alignment with your purpose, mission, and values? Your retention rate can help answer that question. Pay attention and fix yourself.

Tip 35

CULTURE IS CREATED BY THE BEHAVIOR YOU TOLERATE

You can post placards with uplifting words, your memos and speeches can have soaring ideals, but your demonstrated behavior is what forms a culture. There are valid excuses for occasional gaffes or one-off exceptions, but it is a slippery slope. Soon, off-color jokes become commonplace, whining replaces winning, and respect for others dwindles.

Every manufacturing process has its defects that are a small percentage of error or waste. Good managers work to reduce that number of waste to maximize the output of the asset. This knowledge should be applied to your culture. When you begin demonstrating new behaviors in your culture, there will be errors and misjudgments. Learn from them and make corrections.

Do not tolerate ongoing infractions because these problems reduce your production. Good leaders don't forget to guard and nurture their culture nor allow rust or contaminants to ruin their work. Equally, if your leader regularly sullies the culture with poor behavior of their own, look for a new leader.

Tip 36

BUILD EVERY DAY

A high-performance team will not be built in one day, but you can start today. It takes a while to assemble a team, let alone one that is high performing. You cannot randomly throw people together without any structure or purpose and expect brilliance because you will get dysfunction instead. Start with knowing what success looks like for you, and then build toward that goal.

FINAL TOUGHTS

You do not need positional power to lead well, but to be effective, you can no longer ignore the essential leadership tools that focus on treating people on teams with dignity, respect, and common sense. There is no excuse for taking advantage of people, withholding praise, and leading selfishly. The world requires selfless leaders who understand the value of individual goals and collaborative success. When done well, leading a team can be one of life's rewarding practices. May you embrace your opportunities to manage better and lead well.

About the Author

Karl Bimshas, Boston-bred and California-chilled leadership consultant and author of several books and programs designed for busy professionals who want to manage better and lead well.

With an M.S. in Executive Leadership from the University of San Diego and a B.A. in Mass Communications from Emerson College in Boston, Karl Bimshas has held operational and sales leadership positions in public and private corporations. As a sought-after executive coach and leadership consultant, he's helped busy professionals find, set and get their great goals by discovering the a-ha within.

Want help being a better team leader?

Karl Bimshas Consulting is the leadership development and accountability firm that busy professionals turn to help grow their confidence and support around management and leadership.

For more information, visit
www.KarlBimshasConsulting.com
or call 619-497-2670